God's Amazing Animals

Christine Harder Tangvald
Illustrated by Steve Henry

Chariot Books™ is an imprint of David C. Cook Publishing Co.
David C. Cook Publishing Co., Elgin, Illinois 60120
David C. Cook Publishing Co., Weston, Ontario
Nova Distribution Ltd., Torquay, England
GOD'S AMAZING ANIMALS
©1991 by Christine Harder Tangvald for text and Steve Henry for illustrations.
All rights reserved.
Cover and interior design by Therese Cooper
First Printing, 1991. Printed in the United States of America
95 94 93 92 91 5 4 3 2 1
ISBN 1-55513-679-6   LC 91-70859

Chariot Books™
David C. Cook Publishing Co.

All Scripture quotations in this publication are from the *Holy Bible, New International Version.*
©1973, 1978, 1984, International Bible Society. Used by permission of Zondervan Bible Publishers.

A Nose as Long as a Hose!

HELLO THERE!

My name is **Christine**! What is **your** name?
WOW! I **like** your name.
And I think I will like YOU, too. In fact, **I already do**!

I'm SO GLAD you are going to go through this devotional book with me. We are going to have FUN—lots and lots of fun learning about **God's Amazing Animals**. Shall we get started? Okay. LET'S GO!

Have you actually ever seen a huge, huge ELEPHANT? I have.
One time at a circus, I even got to RIDE on an elephant.
It was scary, but it was FUN.

Elephants are AMAZING animals.
God made them that way.
Our Bible verse says so:

"In wisdom you made them all.
(Psalm 104:24b)

When elephants walk, they STOMP and TROMP,
they SWAGGER and SWAY THIS way . . . then THAT way!
And elephants have **wrinkly skin** that looks like it needs to be ironed!
Their big ears go flop, flop, flop.

But my favorite part of an elephant is his TRUNK. His trunk is his NOSE
And God gave the elephant a nose as long as a hose!
It's true! An elephant's nose is long and round.
It swings and sways and hangs **way** down . . . clear to the ground!

I wonder why God didn't give US a nose as long as a hose?
Would **you** like to have a long, long nose like an elephant?

You could give yourself a FINE SHOWER!

You could smell chocolate chip cookies baking NEXT DOOR without EVER LEAVING YOUR HOUSE!

You could pat yourself on the back—with your VERY OWN NOSE!

And SQUIRT, SQUIRT, SQUIRT. You could put out fires, or be a SPRINKLER!

Yes, it might be FUN to have a nose as long as a hose.

But wouldn't a long, long nose get in the way
if you wanted to kiss someone goodnight?

And what if your nose got an AWFUL ITCH?
That is a **lot** of nose to scratch, scratch, SCRATCH!

And what if you tried to **smell** a teeny-tiny flower?
SNIFFLE, SNIFFLE—SNORK!
And you sucked it **right in**!
Where did that flower go?

And what if you got a **bad cold** or **hay fever**?
Oh, dear. Oh, my.
KerSNEEZE . . . KerWHEEZE . . . KerCHOOO!

No, I'm glad God didn't give me a nose as long as a hose, aren't you? I like my nice, little **short** nose just fine! But I'm glad God made elephants with noses as long as hoses. I really like God's elephants. I like them a lot.

PRAYER TIME

Dear God,
Thank You for Your AMAZING elephants with long, long noses. And thank You for short, SHORT noses . . . like MINE!
Amen

GOOD-BYE TIME

Wasn't this FUN? Next time, we will talk about another one of God's amazing animals. You know, YOU are amazing, too. God made you that way, and He did a VERY GOOD JOB! See you next time. Good-bye!

SOMETHING FUN-TO-DO

1. Very carefully, cut out the **Beautiful Bible Bookmark** in the back of this book. Have someone help you find Psalm 104:24b in your very own Bible. Put your Beautiful Bible Bookmark **right there**—at Psalm 104:24b—so you can find this verse again.

2. Cut out your ELEPHANT stand-up figure in the front of this book. Open this book to GOD'S AMAZING ANIMALS ZOO, pages 22 and 23. Stand up your elephant to start your zoo. Each time we will add another amazing animal.

3. ELEPHANT WALK: Clasp your hands together and bend over. Pretend you are a BIG, HEAVY ELEPHANT. Your arms are the elephant's trunk. Make your arms hang way, way down and swing and sway as you **tromp** and stomp around. Lean THIS way, then THAT way . . . swing and sway. STOMP AND TROMP! Have FUN, big elephant!

A Terrific Tail!

HELLO TIME

Hi, there!

How are you today? Did you have fun doing the ELEPHANT WALK? I did. And I can hardly **wait** to learn about another one of GOD'S AMAZING ANIMALS . . . with YOU. Here we go!

Have you ever seen a MONKEY climb a tree? ZIP, ZIP, ZOOM! . . . WOW! They go **fast**.

I love to watch monkeys, don't you? Monkeys have so much FUN! They **chatter** and **screech**—and use their arms to **reach** for branches as they swing through trees in the jungle.

ZIP, ZIP, ZOOM—They swing here.
ZIP, ZIP, ZOOM—They swing there.
ZIP, ZIP, ZOOM—Monkeys swing EVERYWHERE!

Monkeys are AMAZING animals. God made them that way.

Our Bible verse says so:

VERSE TIME

"In wisdom you made them all."
(Psalm 104:24b)

Can you find this verse in your Bible?

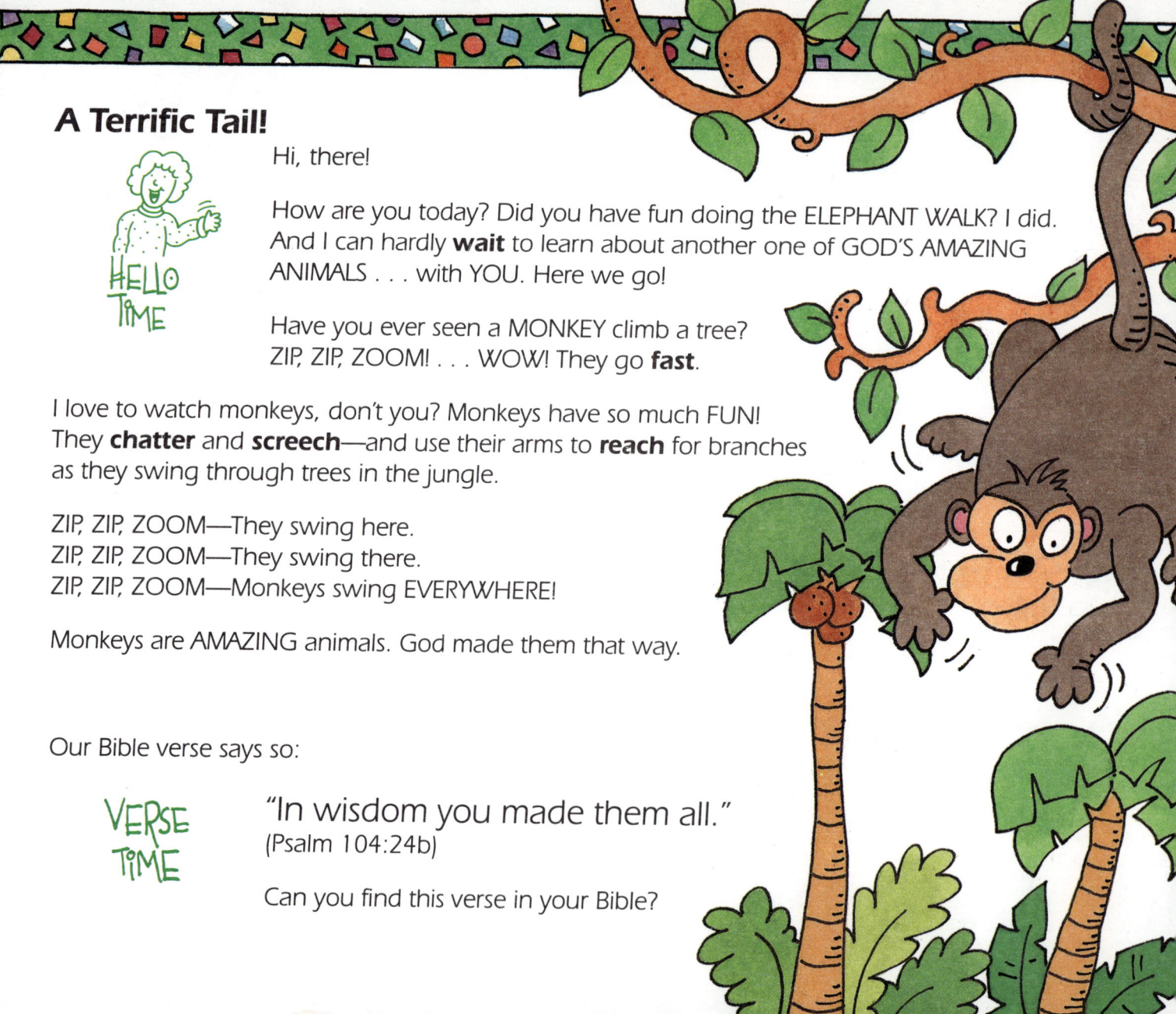

Some monkeys wrap their tails around branches high in a tree and HANG UPSIDE DOWN! And they **do not fall** . . . **at all**!

Do you think it would be fun to have a TAIL like a monkey and HANG UPSIDE DOWN? I do! If **you** had a neat, nifty tail—

You could HANG AROUND anywhere!

You could climb a tree **faster** than anybody in your family!

You could use your tail like a LASSO! Swoosh, swoosh, whoosh . . . GOTCHA!

You could **decorate** your tail with bows and rings and all sorts of things! Doesn't that look splendid?—simply splendid!?

You could really, really **swing** on the monkey bars at the park . .

WHEEEE! Watch ME!

And you could "**hold tails**" with your best friend!

BUT...
If you had a tail, wouldn't it be hard to SIT DOWN?

And would your tail fit inside your **clothes**?

Mean people might pull on your tail . . . or **step on it**!
And it would hurt . . . A LOT!

And what if you accidentally got your tail caught
in an ELEVATOR DOOR!
Crunch . . . ooooch . . . OUCH!

Oh, NO. I do not think I **want** a tail, do you? I don't NEED one. But I am glad God put tails on monkeys, because monkeys DO need their tails to swing through trees in the jungle.

Isn't God WISE? He made everything exactly right.

VERSE TIME

Dear God,
Monkeys are AMAZING! You made them that way.
I like Your amazing monkeys, God.
Thank You for making monkeys like monkeys,
and thank You for making ME like ME!
Amen

GOOD-BYE TIME

Are we finished already? I was having so much FUN!
Well, we will just have to get together **next time** and have some MORE FUN learning about GOD'S AMAZING ANIMALS!

See you then. Good-bye!

SOMETHING FUN-TO-DO

1. Cut out your MONKEY stand-up figure from the front of this book. Set him up with your elephant on your GOD'S AMAZING ANIMALS ZOO.

2. MONKEY WALK: Monkeys walk on their back legs, but they use their arms for support. Bend your knees just enough so your fingers touch the floor in front of you. Now, pretend to WALK LIKE A MONKEY! **Have fun**.

Slither, Slither Slide!

Hello, again! It's so nice to see you. Are you ready to have some MORE FUN learning about GOD'S AMAZING ANIMALS? You are? Good. Let's get started.

Slither, slither, SLIDE! Slither, slither, SLIDE!
Alligators are AMAZING creatures to see. God made them that way.

Our Bible verse says so:

"In wisdom you made them all."
(Psalm 104:24b)

Alligators slither and slide on the muddy banks of swamps and marshes. Slither, slither, SLIDE! Slither, slither, SLIDE!

Then, SPLASH! they use their long, powerful tails to help them slither and glide through the murky water.

Slither, slither, GLIDE! Slither, slither, GLIDE!

Alligators have leathery skin and horny scales, and they like to lie in the hot, hot sun.

And alligators have ENORMOUS mouths with jaws that open wide—
and lots and lots of
GREAT HUGE TEETH!

I wonder why God didn't give us enormous mouths and lots and lots of
GREAT HUGE TEETH!

If **you** had an ENORMOUS MOUTH with lots and lots of teeth
like an alligator, just think of all the FOOD you could EAT!

You could eat 16 **candy bars** all at once!
Crunch, crunch, CRUNCH!
Munch, munch, MUNCH!

You could eat a WHOLE WATERMELON!
Gulp—gulp—SLURP!

You could eat a WHOLE CHOCOLATE CAKE!
Gulp—gulp—SLURP!

You could eat a HUGE BANANA SPLIT, made with
5 gallons of ice cream   **2 quarts** of strawberry syrup
1 dozen bananas   **1 pint** of whipped cream, and
2 quarts of chocolate syrup **100** cherries on the top

Gulp—gulp—SLURP! Gulp—gulp—BURP!

BUT . . .
if you ate ALL that candy and ice cream, you MIGHT get **cavities** in all those teeth!
OUCH!

And you would have to brush and brush and brush, and floss and floss and floss your teeth for at **least** an **hour**!

Well, GUESS WHAT!
I don't think I **want** to eat 16 candy bars all at one time,
and I don't **want** to eat a whole watermelon,
or a whole chocolate cake in one GULP!
And I don't **want** to eat 5 gallons of ice cream
with a dozen bananas in one SLURP!

Do you know why?
If I ate **that** much food **that** fast,
I would get a **GIANT BELLYACHE**!

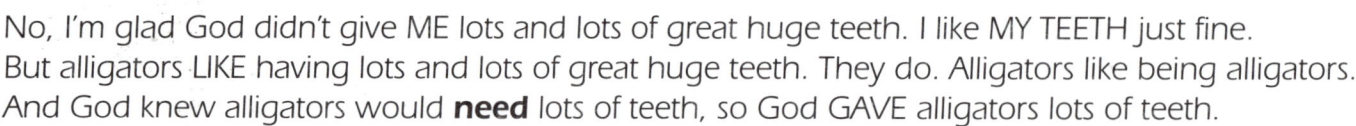

No, I'm glad God didn't give ME lots and lots of great huge teeth. I like MY TEETH just fine.
But alligators LIKE having lots and lots of great huge teeth. They do. Alligators like being alligators.
And God knew alligators would **need** lots of teeth, so God GAVE alligators lots of teeth.

Isn't God wise?

PRAYER TIME

Dear God,
I am glad You are WISE. You knew an alligator would **need** all those teeth, and You knew I DIDN'T!
Thank You for alligators that go SLITHER, SLITHER, **SLIDE**!
God, I think Your alligators are AMAZING!
Amen

GOOD-BYE TIME

God **did** make some AMAZING ANIMALS, didn't He? I can hardly wait until next time to see which amazing animal we will learn about then. (Don't peek!) See you then.
Good-bye!

SOMETHING FUN-TO-DO

1. Cut out your ALLIGATOR stand-up figure. Set him up with your elephant and monkey on your GOD'S AMAZING ANIMALS ZOO.

2. SLITHER, SLITHER, SLIDE! Pretend you are an alligator. Lie on the floor on your tummy. Use your arms and elbows to pull, pull, pull. Push, push, push with your knees.
Slither, slither, SLIDE! Slither, slither, SLIDE!

Have FUN!

Skyscraper Neck!

Hi, there! Are you having a good day? I hope so.

Did you have fun yesterday going slither, slither, slide like an ALLIGATOR? I did. Aren't alligators **amazing**?

Our Bible verse says so:

"In wisdom you made them all."
(Psalm 104:24b)

Can you find our verse in YOUR Bible?

Today we are going to talk about another one of GOD'S AMAZING ANIMALS . . . the GIRAFFE.

The giraffe is one of God's **most** amazing animals. Giraffes have long, long, long, long, long, long, long, long, long, long NECKS! Yes, they do! In fact, giraffes have the longest necks in the whole wide world. God made them that way.

And do you know what?
His HEAD sits clear up there on the **tip top** of that long, long neck! Isn't that AMAZING? The giraffe's head is so high in the sky that he can eat leaves off the top of tall, tall trees!

Can you guess what a giraffe's **favorite food** is to eat? He absolutely LOVES to eat . . . leaves off the tops of TALL, TALL TREES!

Isn't that **handy** and **dandy** since his head is already UP THERE?

Do **you** think it would be **fun** to be a giraffe?

If YOU had a neck that long, just **think** of the things you could DO!

You could peek into the window on the top floor of a HOTEL.

You could say "BOO!" to a buzzard that was flying by.

You could see a PARADE even if you were stuck behind lots and lots of TALL PEOPLE!

Oh, yes, it might be FUN to be a giraffe . . . for a while!

But do you think it would be fun to be a giraffe if . . .

You wanted to go for a **ride** in the car with your mom?

Or if you wanted to eat some chocolate ice cream with a spoon?

Or if you wanted to sleep in your VERY OWN BED?

And what if you got a SORE THROAT? Oh, dear, oh my. You'd have a SORE THROAT clear up to the SKY!

Then it would **not** be fun to be a giraffe, would it?

But GUESS WHAT! A giraffe does not sleep in a bed, or ride in a car, or eat chocolate ice cream with a spoon.

A giraffe lives in the forest, and eats leaves off TALL, TALL TREES. That's why God gave the giraffe such a long, long, long, long, long, long, long, long NECK!

Isn't that AMAZING!

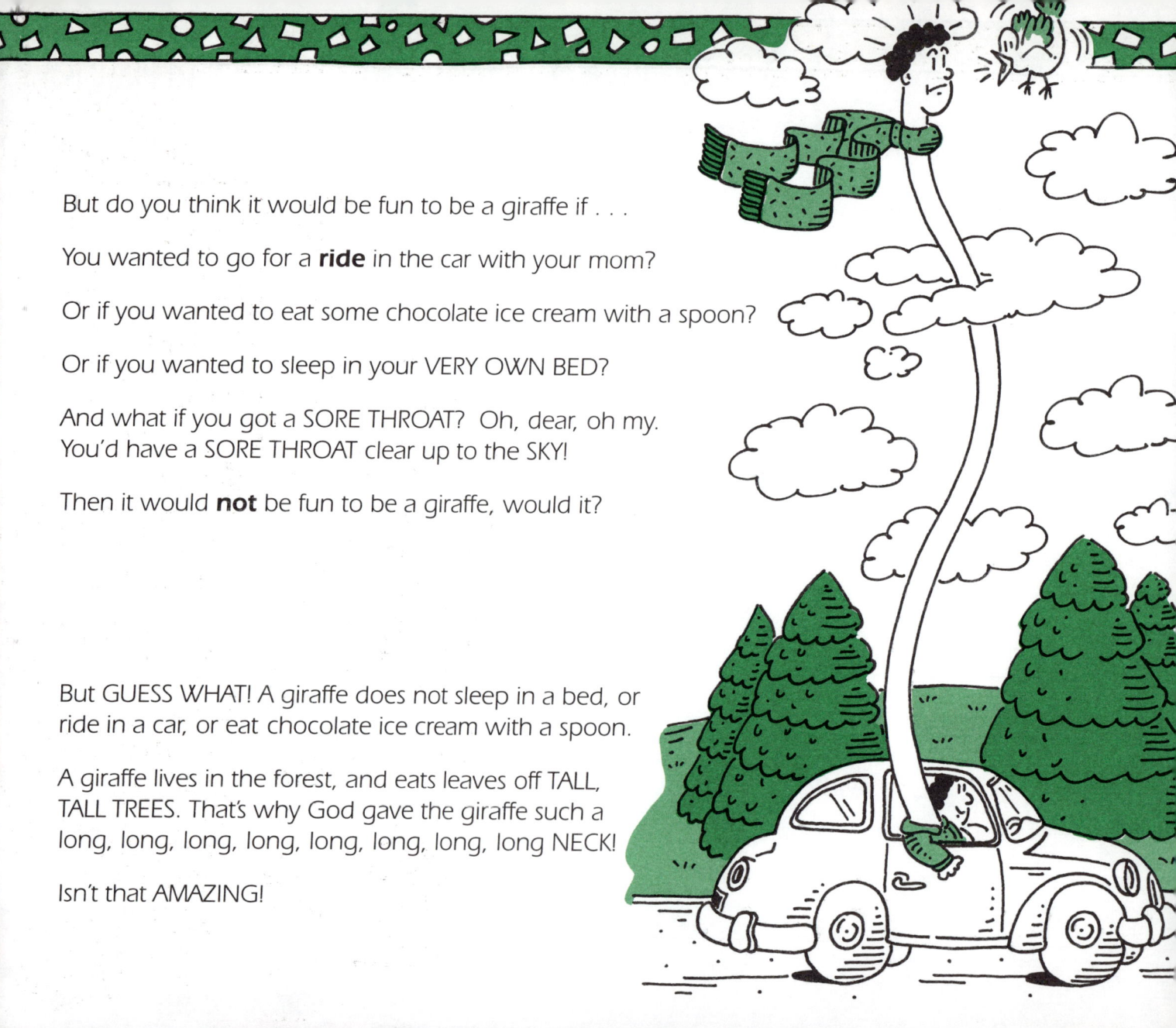

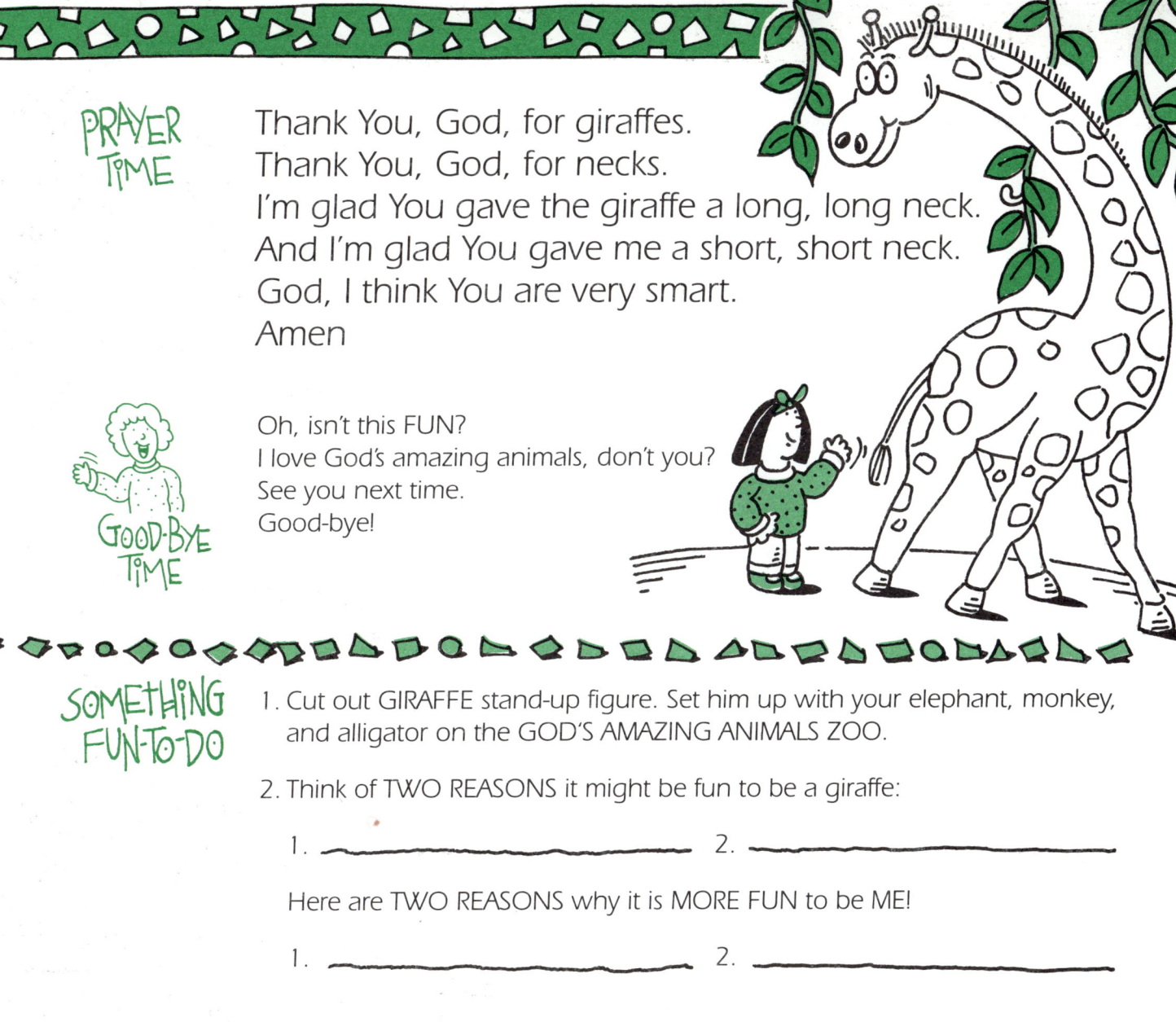

PRAYER TIME

Thank You, God, for giraffes.
Thank You, God, for necks.
I'm glad You gave the giraffe a long, long neck.
And I'm glad You gave me a short, short neck.
God, I think You are very smart.
Amen

GOOD-BYE TIME

Oh, isn't this FUN?
I love God's amazing animals, don't you?
See you next time.
Good-bye!

SOMETHING FUN-TO-DO

1. Cut out GIRAFFE stand-up figure. Set him up with your elephant, monkey, and alligator on the GOD'S AMAZING ANIMALS ZOO.

2. Think of TWO REASONS it might be fun to be a giraffe:

   1. _____ 2. _____

   Here are TWO REASONS why it is MORE FUN to be ME!

   1. _____ 2. _____

KerBOING, KerBOING, KerBOING

HELLO!

I hope you are as **excited** as I am to learn about another one of GOD'S AMAZING ANIMALS.
You are? Oh, good.
Here we go!

KerBOING, KerBOING, Ker**BOING**!

Do you know what kind of animal God made that goes **KerBOING**?
This animal does not run.
This animal does not walk.

THIS animal LEAPS and BOUNCES and HOPS through the air . . . everywhere it goes!

KerBOING, KerBOING, Ker**BOING**!

And not only that. This amazing animal has a pocket right in its **tummy** called a POUCH. Do you know what she carries inside her pouch?

Oh, WAIT! I forgot to **tell** you what kind of amazing animal goes KerBOING, KerBOING, Ker**BOING**!

Did you guess that it is a KANGAROO?

And have you guessed what a kangaroo carries inside her handy dandy POUCH? She carries a BABY in there! A BABY KANGAROO! Isn't that amazing?

God made her that way, you know. Our Bible verse says so:

VERSE TIME "In wisdom you made them all."
(Psalm 104:24b)

Do YOU think it would be FUN to be a kangaroo?
To have a handy dandy **pouch** in your tummy—and to **leap** and **bounce** and **hop** through the air . . . EVERYWHERE?
KerBOING, KerBOING, Ker**BOING**!

You could make **lots** of points in a BASKETBALL GAME.
Kerboing . . . SLAM, DUNK . . . Swish!

You could get things for your mother OFF THE TOP SHELF!
KerBOING . . . grab . . .

You could carry some **chewing gum** in your pouch. And some crayons and some marbles and your yellow Yo-Yo! And a peanut-butter sandwich or some crackers and cheese. You could even make your very own milkshake.
KerBOING . . . KerBOING . . . KerBOING!

Yes, that might be FUN!

But, it might NOT be fun to be a KANGAROO in a room with a very LOW CEILING!

KerBOING . . . BUMP . . . BONK!
KerBOING . . . THUMP . . . BONK!

And I don't think it would be fun to be the poor BABY KANGAROO bouncing around all day inside my mother's pouch—OUCH!

What a bumpy ride!

No, I do not want to leap and hop through the air everywhere I go.
I'm glad God gave **me** two nice **legs** to walk and run on, aren't you?

But I really LIKE God's amazing kangaroos.
You see, God made kangaroos **exactly** the way HE wants THEM to be.
And God made YOU **exactly** the way HE wants YOU to be.
God is so wise.

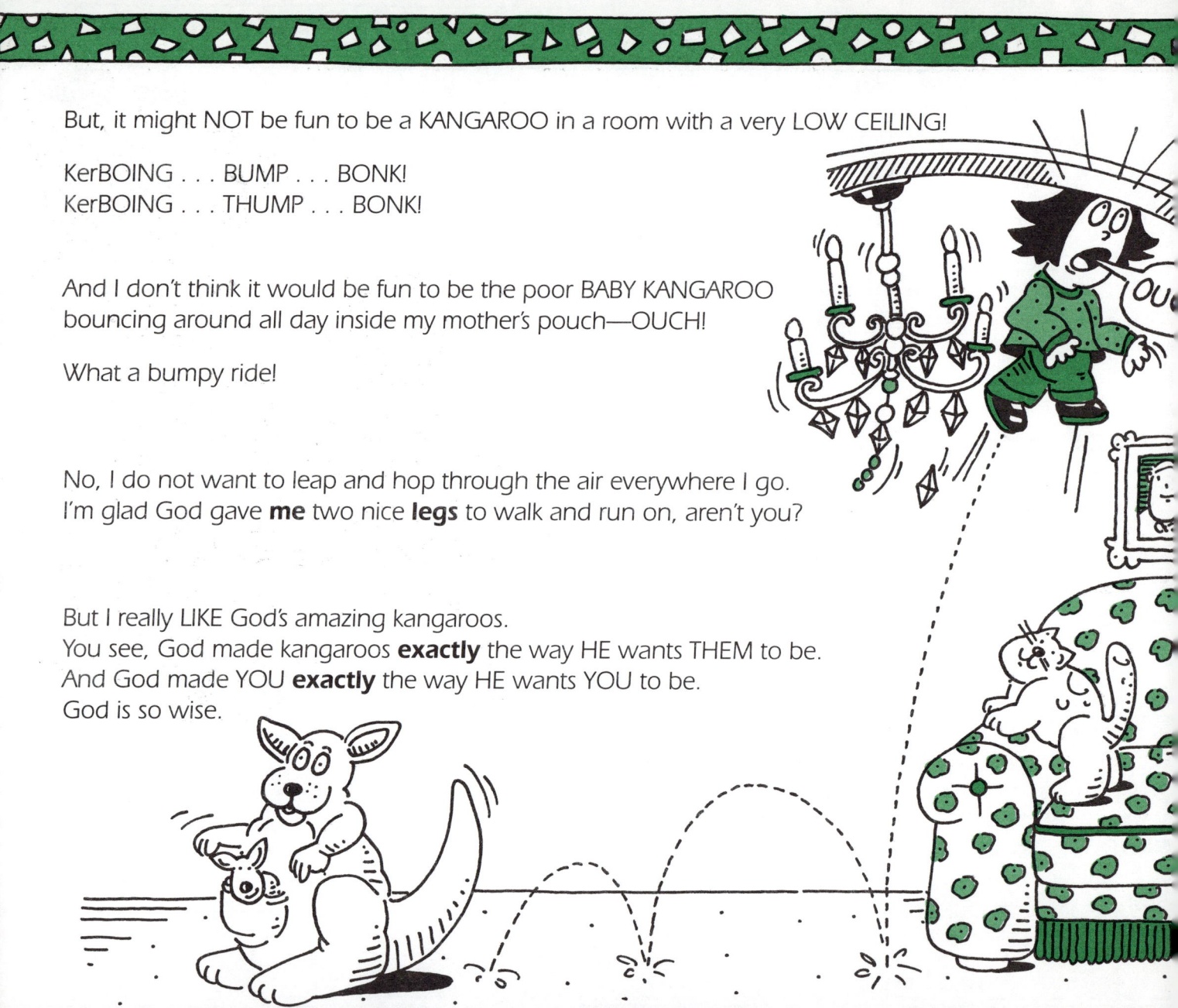

 PRAYER TIME

Dear God,
I think Your kangaroos are WONDERFUL.
And, God, I think YOU are **wonderful**, too.
Thank You for making **everything** exactly right!
Amen

 GOOD-BYE TIME

Going through this book with **you** has been SO MUCH FUN! I am sad it is over.

Maybe we can go through another Fun-To-Do book together sometime. I'd like that. But for now, I have to say good-bye. But always remember:
I think YOU are NICE. VERY, VERY NICE!
Good-bye from your SPECIAL FRIEND,

 SOMETHING FUN-TO-DO

1. Cut out the KANGAROO stand-up figure, and set it up with all the other animals on your GOD'S AMAZING ANIMALS ZOO.

2. KANGAROO HOP: Bend your knees and squat way down. Hold your hands in front of you like little paws. Now, LEAP and HOP and BOUNCE through the air . . . EVERYWHERE! Have fun!

1. Cut out all the AMAZING ANIMALS stand-up figures from the front and back of this book—one for each devotion.

2. Place each animal in its own home in GOD'S AMAZING ANIMALS ZOO

3. Keep this zoo page open on top of a table, your dresser, or some other place where you will see it often. Have FUN!

Maybe . . . sometime . . . you can go to a REAL zoo and see more of God's AMAZING ANIMALS. Wouldn't that be FUN?

Dear Parents,

I'm so glad you have chosen this Fun-to-Do Devotions book to do with your child and with **me**! You won't need much time to go through these fun devotions, but be sure the time is as regular as possible—maybe after a meal or after nap time.

You don't need many things to start out, just this book and the Bible and whatever the devotion suggests to make it a really fun time for you and your child.

Each devotion uses the same elements. In each one you'll find:
- HELLO TIME
- PRAYER TIME
- VERSE TIME
- GOOD-BYE TIME
- SOMETHING FUN TO DO

Because young children learn well through repetition, the same Scripture verse is used in each devotion. By the time you finish this book, your child will probably have memorized the verse.

When you finish this book, look for more Fun-to-Do Devotions at your local Christian bookstore.

I promise—these devotions will be fun for both you and your child!

God Bless!

Christine